# USING MATHS
# BUILD A SKYSCRAPER

by Hilary Koll, Steve Mills
and William Baker

ticktock

# USING
# MATHS
## BUILD A SKYSCRAPER

Copyright © ticktock Entertainment Ltd 2006

First published in Great Britain in 2006 by ticktock Media Ltd.,
Unit 2, Orchard Business Centre, North Farm Road, Tunbridge Wells, Kent, TN2 3XF

ISBN 1 86007 986 5
Printed in China

### HILARY KOLL

Hilary Koll (B.Ed. Hons) was a Leading Maths Teacher in a primary school before training as a Numeracy Consultant for the National Numeracy Strategy. She has worked as a Lecturer in Mathematics Education at the University of Reading, teaching on undergraduate, post-graduate and training courses. She is now a full-time writer and consultant in mathematics education. Hilary Koll and Steve Mills can be contacted via their website www.cmeprojects.com

### STEVE MILLS

Steve Mills (B.A. Hons, P.G.C.E., M.Ed.) was a teacher of both primary and secondary age children and an LEA Maths Advisory Support Teacher before joining the University of Reading as a Lecturer in Mathematics Education. He worked with both under-graduate and post-graduate students in their preparation for teaching maths in schools. He has written many mathematics books for both teachers and children. Visit www.cmeprojects.com for details.

### WILLIAM BAKER

Bill is in charge of Structural Engineering for Skidmore, Owings & Merrill LLP in Chicago. Bill has developed the structural systems of some of the world's tallest buildings, including the 160 story Burj Dubai, which will be the world's tallest. Bill was also one of the lead investigators of the collapse of the World Trade Center Towers. In addition to his work at SOM, Bill is an adjunct professor at the Illinois Institute of Technology and lectures frequently.

# CONTENTS

## NUMERACY WORK COVERED IN THIS BOOK:

**CALCULATIONS:**
Throughout this book there are opportunities to practise **addition, subtraction, multiplication** and **division** using both mental calculation strategies and pencil and paper methods.

**NUMBERS AND THE NUMBER SYSTEM:**
- COMPARING NUMBERS: pgs. 6, 9, 15, 20
- DECIMALS: pg. 20
- ESTIMATING: pgs. 22, 24, 25
- NEGATIVE NUMBERS: pgs. 16, 17
- ORDERING NUMBERS: pg. 20
- ROUNDING UP AND DOWN: pgs. 12, 20

**SOLVING 'REAL LIFE' PROBLEMS:**
- TIME: pgs. 7, 8, 9, 22, 25
- USING CALENDARS: pg. 24

**HANDLING DATA:**
- GRAPHS: pg. 9
- TABLES: pgs. 7, 27
- USING FORMULAS: pgs. 11, 27

**MEASURES:**
- CONVERTING METRIC/IMPERIAL MEASUREMENTS: pg. 26

**SHAPE AND SPACE:**
- 2-D SHAPES: pgs. 10, 12, 18
- 3-D SHAPES: pgs. 14, 15
- ANGLES: pg. 18
- AREA: pgs. 10, 11, 12, 14, 26
- LINE SYMMETRY: pg. 18
- PERIMETER: pgs. 10, 12
- VOLUME: pgs. 14, 15

**Supports the maths work taught at Key Stage 2 and 3**

# HOW TO USE THIS BOOK

**M**aths is important in the lives of people everywhere. We use maths when we play a game, ride a bike, go shopping - in fact, all the time! Everyone needs to use maths at work. You may not realise it, but an architect would use maths when designing a skyscraper! With this book you will get the chance to try lots of exciting maths activities using real life data and facts about tall buildings. Practise your maths and numeracy skills and experience the thrill of what it's really like to design and build a skyscraper.

**This exciting maths book is very easy to use – check out what's inside!**

Fun to read information about how skyscrapers are built.

## MATHS ACTIVITIES

Look for the **SKYSCRAPER WORK.** You will find real life maths activities and questions to try.

To answer some of the questions, you will need to collect data from a DATA BOX. Sometimes, you will need to collect facts and data from the text or from charts and diagrams.

Be prepared! You will need a pen or pencil and a notebook for your workings and answers.

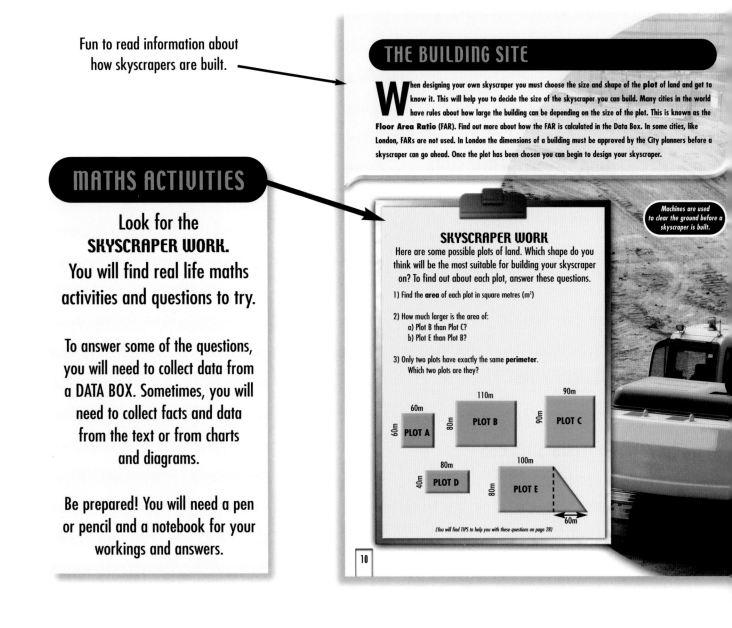

### THE BUILDING SITE

**W**hen designing your own skyscraper you must choose the size and shape of the **plot** of land and get to know it. This will help you to decide the size of the skyscraper you can build. Many cities in the world have rules about how large the building can be depending on the size of the plot. This is known as the **Floor Area Ratio (FAR)**. Find out more about how the FAR is calculated in the Data Box. In some cities, like London, FARs are not used. In London the dimensions of a building must be approved by the City planners before a skyscraper can go ahead. Once the plot has been chosen you can begin to design your skyscraper.

*Machines are used to clear the ground before a skyscraper is built.*

### SKYSCRAPER WORK

Here are some possible plots of land. Which shape do you think will be the most suitable for building your skyscraper on? To find out about each plot, answer these questions.

1) Find the **area** of each plot in square metres (m²)

2) How much larger is the area of:
   a) Plot B than Plot C
   b) Plot E than Plot B?

3) Only two plots have exactly the same **perimeter**. Which two plots are they?

PLOT A — 60m, 60m
PLOT B — 110m, 80m
PLOT C — 90m, 90m
PLOT D — 80m, 40m
PLOT E — 100m, 80m, 60m

*(You will find TIPS to help you with these questions on page 28)*

10

If you see one of these boxes, there will be important data inside that will help you with the maths activities.

Feeling confident? Try these extra **CHALLENGE QUESTIONS.**

## DATA BOX

### FLOOR AREA RATIO

Many cities use a rule to decide how much building is allowed on plots of different sizes. The rule they use is called the Floor Area Ratio (FAR).

To calculate this, first find the area of the plot. Then multiply the answer by the FAR number for the city you want to build in. In New York, a high FAR number is 18.
The answer gives you the maximum floor area of the building that you can sell or rent out (not including basements, mechanical space, roofs and parking).
If your plot area in New York is 10,000 m² you could rent out 180,000 m². If your building had 100 **storeys**, each could perhaps have a floor area on average of about 1800 m².

In Chicago, FARs are sometimes as high as 34. This is why Chicago has more of the supertall towers.

# IF YOU NEED HELP...

## TIPS FOR MATHS SUCCESS

On pages 28 – 29 you will find lots of tips to help you with your maths work.

## ANSWERS

Turn to pages 30 – 31 to check your answers.
(Try all the activities and questions before you take a look at the answers.)

## GLOSSARY

On page 32 there is a glossary of skyscraper words and a glossary of maths words. The glossary words appear **in bold** in the text.

### CHALLENGE QUESTIONS

Look at the information about the Floor Area Ratio in the DATA BOX above. Use this and your answers to question 1 of the skyscraper work.

If the Floor Area Ratio number is 17.5, what is the maximum floor area that could be rented out for a building on
a) Plot A?
b) Plot B?
c) Plot C?
d) Plot D?
e) Plot E?

11

### FOUNDATION FACTS

When a skyscraper is to be built on really soft soil, a foundation, called a floating raft, is made. For this, a large hole is dug so that the weight of the soil removed equals the weight of the building. This means that the final **load** on the soil does not change and the building will stand firm.

Skyscrapers are very heavy! For example, the Taipai 101 Tower is said to weigh 700 000 tonnes which is 700 million kilograms.

Fun to read facts and tips about how architects, designers and builders work.

# KNOW YOUR SKYSCRAPERS

**Y**ou have been asked to design a skyscraper for a multi-national bank with a budget of £500 million. It should be one of the tallest in the world, perhaps about 400 metres high, and should be able to withstand high winds and earthquakes. You'll need to know about other skyscrapers in the world; their height, shape and how long they have been standing. There will be a lot of interest in your skyscraper, so you will need to think about its shape as well as its height. Tall buildings are being planned and built all the time. One of the biggest is Burj Dubai, a 160 **storey** 'scraper which is being built in the United Arab Emirates at the moment. It's due to be completed in 2008.

## SKYSCRAPER WORK

In the DATA BOX on page 7 you will see facts about some of the tallest skyscrapers in the world. Use the information to help you answer these questions.

1) Which skyscraper in this list:
   a) is tallest?
   b) is oldest?
   c) has the most storeys?

2) How many more storeys has:
   a) the Taipei 101 Tower than the Sky Central Plaza?
   b) the Sears Tower than the Petronas Twin Towers?
   c) the Jin Mao Building than the Bank of China Tower?
   d) the Sears Tower than Shun Hing Square?
   e) the Empire State Building than Two International Finance Centre?

3) How much taller is:
   a) Petronas Twin Towers than the Sears Tower?
   b) Sky Central Plaza than Central Plaza?
   c) Taipei 101 Tower than the Sears Tower?
   d) Two International Finance Centre than Sky Central Plaza ?
   e) Shun Hing Square than the Bank of China Tower?

*(You will find a TIP to help you with these questions on page 28)*

**International Finance Centre**

**Taipai 101 Tower, Taiwan**

# THE WORLD'S TALLEST SKYSCRAPERS

| Name | Location | Year completed | Number of storeys | Height in metres |
|---|---|---|---|---|
| Bank of China Tower | Hong Kong, China | 1989 | 70 | 369 |
| Central Plaza | Hong Kong, China | 1992 | 78 | 374 |
| Empire State Building | New York, USA | 1931 | 102 | 381 |
| Jin Mao Building | Shanghai, China | 1999 | 88 | 421 |
| Petronas Twin Towers | Kuala Lumpur, Malaysia | 1998 | 88 | 452 |
| Sears Tower | Chicago, USA | 1974 | 110 | 442 |
| Shun Hing Square | Shenzhen, China | 1996 | 69 | 384 |
| Sky Central Plaza | Guanzhou, China | 1997 | 80 | 391 |
| Taipei 101 Tower | Taipei, Taiwan | 2004 | 101 | 509 |
| Two International Finance Centre | Hong Kong, China | 2003 | 88 | 415 |

*Many cities, such as Atlanta, USA, can be recognised by the shape their skyscrapers make on the skyline.*

## SPIRE FACTS

The Taipei 101 Tower and the Petronas Twin Towers are considered the world's tallest buildings, but both get much of their height from **spires**. If you don't count the spires, then the Sears Tower is taller than either of these.

The Empire State Building was built with amazing speed – it took just 18 months. Its spire was meant as a place to tie airships to.

The Chrysler Building hid its spire as long as possible because it was competing against another skyscraper. At the last minute, the spire was jacked up from inside the building.

## CHALLENGE QUESTION

Use the information in the DATA BOX to help you answer this questions.

1) How many years after the Empire State building was built were each of these skyscrapers built?
   a) Taipei 101 Tower
   b) Petronas Twin Towers
   c) Sears Tower
   d) Jin Mao Building
   e) Two International Finance Centre
   f) Sky Central Plaza
   g) Shun Hing Square
   h) Central Plaza
   i) Bank of China Tower

2) Now write each of your answers in months.

# RECORD-BREAKING SKYSCRAPERS

f you're going to build a skyscraper, you should know about their history. The word 'skyscraper' was first used in the 18th century to mean a high-flying flag on a ship. The first time it was used to describe buildings was in the 1880s. Large structures were built for special purposes in the past, but the Home Insurance building, in Chicago, built in 1885, is often considered to be the first skyscraper. This is because it was the first to have a steel **frame** or lifts. On this page, find out about what were the tallest buildings in the world at different times in the last century and before. How many of these buildings have you heard of or seen?

## SKYSCRAPER WORK

In the DATA BOX on page 9 you will see a graph showing information about the tallest buildings in the world during the last 100 years or so. Use it to help you answer these questions:

1) About how tall is:
   a) the Chrysler Building?
   b) the Sears Tower?

2) Which building in the graph is about:
   a) 415 m tall?
   b) 380 m tall?
   c) 510 m tall?

3) Which building was the tallest in the world in:
   a) 1980?
   b) 2000?
   c) 1960?
   d) 1970?
   e) 2005?

*The Chrysler Building is lit up at night.*

## TALL BUILDINGS IN HISTORY

Making tall buildings began thousands of years ago. Between 2600 BC and 2570 BC, the Red **Pyramid** in Egypt held the record for the tallest building in the world at 105m tall.

The Great Pyramid was then built in Giza, Egypt, which was 41m taller than the Red Pyramid, and this held the record for the world's tallest building for nearly 4000 years, from 2570 BC until AD 1300! Between 2570 BC and AD 1439 the Great Pyramid eroded, losing approximately 7m from its height.

Lincoln Cathedral in England was completed in 1300 and its wooden **spire** took the record up to 160 metres. This record stood for more than two centuries, until the spire collapsed in 1549.

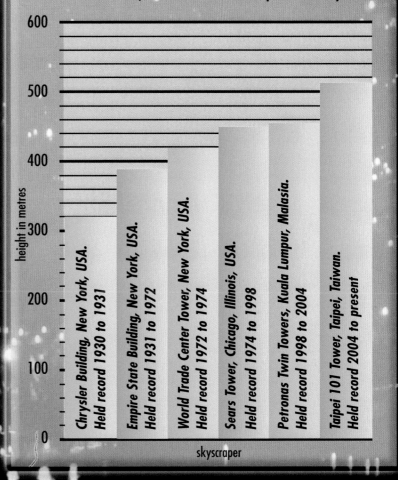

SKYSCRAPERS OF THE PAST

The record holders for the tallest buildings in the world, from 1930 to the present day

height in metres

600

500

400

300

200

100

0

Chrysler Building, New York, USA.
Held record 1930 to 1931

Empire State Building, New York, USA.
Held record 1931 to 1972

World Trade Center Tower, New York, USA.
Held record 1972 to 1974

Sears Tower, Chicago, Illinois, USA.
Held record 1974 to 1998

Petronas Twin Towers, Kuala Lumpur, Malasia.
Held record 1998 to 2004

Taipei 101 Tower, Taipei, Taiwan.
Held record 2004 to present

skyscraper

## CHALLENGE QUESTION

1) In 1930, the Chrysler Building was the tallest building in the world. How many years after 1930 did the following buildings become the tallest building:
   a) the Petronas Twin Towers?
   b) the Empire State Building?
   c) Taipai 101 Tower?
   d) the World Trade Center?
   e) the Sears Tower?

2) About how much taller is:
   a) the Empire State Building than the Chrysler Building?
   b) the Sears Tower than the Empire State Building?
   c) the Petronas Twin Towers than the Sears Tower?
   d) the Taipai 101 Tower than the Petronas Twin Towers?

*(You will find a TIP to help you with these questions on page 28)*

# THE BUILDING SITE

**W**hen designing your own skyscraper you must choose the size and shape of the **plot** of land and get to know it. This will help you to decide the size of the skyscraper you can build. Many cities in the world have rules about how large the building can be depending on the size of the plot. This is known as the **Floor Area Ratio** (FAR). Find out more about how the FAR is calculated in the Data Box. In some cities, like London, FARs are not used. In London the dimensions of a building must be approved by the City planners before a skyscraper can go ahead. Once the plot has been chosen you can begin to design your skyscraper.

*Machines are used to clear the ground before a skyscraper is built.*

## SKYSCRAPER WORK

Here are some possible plots of land. Which shape do you think will be the most suitable for building your skyscraper on? To find out about each plot, answer these questions.

1) Find the **area** of each plot in square metres (m²)

2) How much larger is the area of:
   a) Plot B than Plot C?
   b) Plot E than Plot B?

3) Only two plots have exactly the same **perimeter**.
   Which two plots are they?

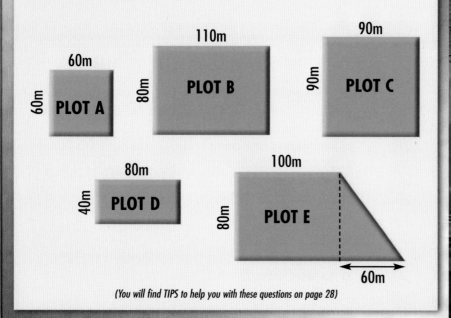

60m
60m
**PLOT A**

110m
80m
**PLOT B**

90m
90m
**PLOT C**

80m
40m
**PLOT D**

100m
80m
**PLOT E**
60m

*(You will find TIPS to help you with these questions on page 28)*

# FLOOR AREA RATIO

Many cities use a rule to decide how much building is allowed on plots of different sizes. The rule they use is called the Floor Area Ratio (FAR).

To calculate this, first find the area of the plot. Then multiply the answer by the FAR number for the city you want to build in. In New York, a high FAR number is 18.

The answer gives you the maximum floor area of the building that you can sell or rent out (not including basements, mechanical space, roofs and parking).

If your plot area in New York is 10,000 m² you could rent out 180,000 m². If your building had 100 **storeys**, each could perhaps have a floor area on average of about 1800 m².

In Chicago, FARs are sometimes as high as 34. This is why Chicago has more of the supertall towers.

## FOUNDATION FACTS

When a skyscraper is to be built on really soft soil, a foundation, called a floating raft, is made. For this, a large hole is dug so that the weight of the soil removed equals the weight of the building. This means that the final **load** on the soil does not change and the building will stand firm.

Skyscrapers are very heavy! For example, the Taipai 101 Tower is said to weigh 700 000 tonnes which is 700 million kilograms.

## CHALLENGE QUESTIONS

Look at the information about the Floor Area Ratio in the DATA BOX above. Use this and your answers to question 1 of the skyscraper work.

If the Floor Area Ratio number is 17.5, what is the maximum floor area that could be rented out for a building on
a) Plot A?
b) Plot B?
c) Plot C?
d) Plot D?
e) Plot E?

# THE SKYSCRAPER'S STRENGTH

**N**ow that you've decided on your **plot** of land and the size of the floor **area**, you'll need to start thinking about what building materials you will need for your skyscraper. Which materials will you use? You will need something very strong. You could use 'reinforced concrete', which is concrete with steel bars inside. It is very strong and the concrete stops the steel bars from weakening in a fire. Usually a steel skeleton for the whole structure is built like putting together a giant construction set. Wood and masonry can only be used for buildings less than about 15 **storeys** as they have limited strength.

## SKYSCRAPER WORK

Here are plans of buildings seen from above.
1) Find the exact **perimeter** of these buildings and then round your answers to the nearest 10 metres.
2) Round the length and width of each building to the nearest 10 metres and use these approximations to **estimate** the areas of these buildings.

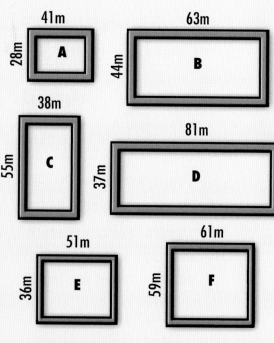

*(You will find TIPS to help you with these questions on page 28)*

## CHALLENGE QUESTION

A building has a perimeter of 200 m. What are the length and width of the building if its area is:
a) 2500 m²
b) 2400 m²
c) 1600 m²
d) 900 m²
e) 2475 m²
f) 475 m²
g) 2499 m²

*(You will find a TIP to help you with this question on page 28)*

## CONCRETE FACTS

In a building made of concrete, it usually takes about 1 month for the new concrete to gain its full strength. Concrete is very strong in resisting **compression** (pushing) loads, but weak in resisting **tensile** (pulling) loads.

## SUPPORTING THE SKYSCRAPER

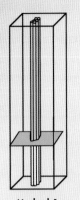

Method 1

Buildings must be strong enough to stand firm in extreme winds. Here are two ways to do this.

### Method 1
Steel or concrete **columns** are built at the centre of the skyscraper so that the building has a 'backbone' a bit like the human body. The tube-shape is very strong and resistant to **torsion** (twist). During construction, the 'backbone' is built first, then the floors and finally the outside of the building. This method means that the floors of the building are light and spacious.

### Method 2
The whole building is one large strong tube, with the steel or concrete **frame** around the outside. Construction usually is done floor-by-floor up the height of the building.

Whatever the method, the last thing to be built is the outer layer of the building, the façade. This is done at the end so that the heavy equipment and cranes do not damage it while the rest of the skyscraper is being built.

Method 2

*Cranes can raise and lower materials quickly and position them with great accuracy.*

# YOUR DESIGN

Skyscrapers come in all shapes and sizes. Since the structures are usually bolted together like a large construction set, the only real limit on the shape and size is the imagination of the architects and engineers who put the pieces together. What shape would you like your skyscraper to be? What do you need to think about when deciding this? The amount of money you have is one factor, and you will also need to know the purpose of your skyscraper. Will it be used as a huge office block or homes for people? How will this affect your design? The building could be a mixture of office, homes and perhaps also include a hotel or shops.

## SKYSCRAPER WORK
Here are some pictures of buildings of different shapes and sizes.

1) Can you name the different shapes that make up each building?
2) Which of the buildings are types of **prisms**?

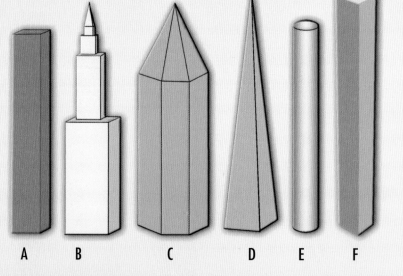

A  B  C  D  E  F

3) a) Building E has a roof **area** of 2000 m² and a height of 350 m. What is the **volume** of the building?
   b) Building F has a roof area of 2000 m² and a height of 400 m. What is the volume of the building?

*(You will find a TIP to help you with these questions on page 28)*

*Most skyscrapers are cuboid in shape, as this view of Chicago, USA shows.*

## CHALLENGE QUESTION

Which of the following cuboid buildings has the greatest volume?

Building A: 390m tall, 55m wide and 60m long
Building B: 360m tall, 50m wide and 61m long
Building C: 420m tall, 52m wide and 55m long

*(You will find a TIP to help you with this question on page 29)*

## DESIGN FACTS

Skyscrapers can be built as offices or as places that people live. If the building is to be **residential**, designers must make sure that the spaces inside are never too far from a window. This is because people like natural light in their homes and enjoy looking out at the view. If the skyscraper is built as offices it is less important for every part to be close to a window as artificial lights are more often used to light up small rooms and cupboards at the centre of the building.

# GOOD FOUNDATIONS

**W**hen you are constructing a tall building you must make sure it is built on solid ground. If you build directly on soil that is too soft, a building would start to lean (subside) or might even fall down. So it is important to dig down under the soft soil to the hard ground underneath. When solid ground has been reached, builders pour in lots of reinforced concrete to make the foundations even firmer and to spread the weight of the building evenly. In soft soil, deep foundations called piles or **caissons** (pronounced kaysons) are used to support a skyscraper. These are like sticks or stilts that go down to strong, solid rock deep in the ground.

*Reinforced concrete is made by pouring concrete over steel bars.*

## SKYSCRAPER WORK

The DATA BOX on page 17 shows a sketch of the lower part of a building. Use the sketch to help you answer these questions.

Which level is:
a) 1 level below Ground floor 0?
b) 4 levels above Basement -2?
c) 5 levels below **Storey** 3?
d) 6 levels above Basement -1?
e) 3 levels below Basement -1?
f) 5 levels above Storey 1?
g) 10 levels above Basement -6?
h) 9 levels below Storey 4?

### FLOOR FACTS

Not all skyscrapers have a floor 13. The number 13 is sometimes considered unlucky, so some skyscrapers call the 13th floor "Floor 14". In China, the number 4 is unlucky, so Chinese buildings often go from "Floor 3" to "Floor 5".

## FOUNDATION FACTS

**Pile foundations** are 'stilts' that reach down to firm ground to support the weight of the building.

Where firm ground does not exist, or it is too deep to reach with piles, a **raft foundation** might be used. This spreads the load from the building onto the surrounding soil. If the load can be spread evenly, the soil under the raft can support the weight of the building.

If the building loads are high, a combination of these two foundations can be used, and the load can be shared between the raft foundation and the piles.

Building with
pile foundation

Building with
raft foundation

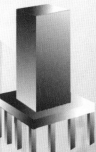

Building with pile
and raft foundation

## CHALLENGE QUESTION

The lift is travelling up and down the building shown in the DATA BOX on page 19.

On which level will the lift be after these movements?
- Starts on Ground level 0.
- Goes up 15 floors
- Then down 20 floors
- Up 3 floors
- Up 20 floors
- Down 2 floors
- Down 17 floors.
- And down 2 floors.
Where is the lift now?

DATA BOX on page 19.

## DATA BOX
# NUMBER OF STOREYS

This skyscraper has 88 floors above ground level and 4 basement levels below ground.

Here is a sketch of the lower part of the building:

| | |
|---|---|
| Floor 16 | |
| Floor 15 | |
| Floor 14 | |
| Floor 13 | |
| Floor 12 | |
| Floor 11 | |
| Floor 10 | |
| Floor 9 | |
| Floor 8 | |
| Floor 7 | |
| Floor 6 | |
| Floor 5 | |
| Floor 4 | |
| Floor 3 | |
| Floor 2 | |
| Floor 1 | |
| Ground floor 0 | Ground |
| Basement -1 | Level |
| Basement -2 | |
| Basement -3 | |
| Basement -4 | |
| Basement -5 | |
| Basement -6 | |

# STRENGTHENING THE STRUCTURE

The overall weight of a skyscraper is supported by its **frame** (see pages 12-13), but each floor also needs to be supported. This is done with steel beams and **girders**. Concrete **columns** or walls can be used as well. Engineers think carefully about the shapes that will be made when the girders, columns and walls are joined together. Some shapes, such as triangles, are much stronger than others. Engineers must get the structure of a skyscraper right, so the building is safe. This means architects can be as imaginative as they like when designing the outside of the building – the outer wall (the **façade**) is decorative and not part of the skyscraper's strength.

## SKYSCRAPER WORK

In DATA BOX 1 you will see the importance of triangles when designing strong structures. There are different types of triangles.

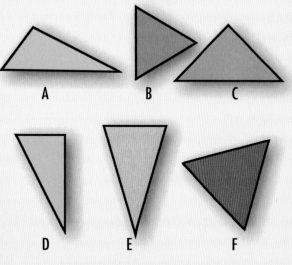

A B C

D E F

1) Can you say whether each of the triangles shown above is **scalene**, **isosceles** or **equilateral**?
2) Which of these triangles have a right-angle?
3) How many lines of reflective symmetry does each triangle have?

*(You will find a TIP to help you with these questions on page 29)*

## CHALLENGE QUESTION

In the DATA BOX 2 you will see some information about the weight per metre of a girder.

Find how heavy a girder is that is:
a) 4.4 metres long
b) 7.2 metres long
c) 11 metres long
d) 14.6 metres long
e) 25.9 metres long

*(You will find a TIP to help you with these questions on page 29)*

## COLUMN FACTS

Steel columns come in many different shapes. They can be "I"-shaped, like girders, or they can be box-shaped or circular-shaped. Concrete columns can be made in many different shapes.

Columns for tall buildings often use steel and concrete together. A steel "I"-shaped column might be encased within a larger concrete column, or a steel box-shaped column might be filled with concrete. Combining these two materials helps to increase the strength and stiffness of the column.

## DATA BOX — GIRDERS

Girders come in different lengths. Girders are commonly shaped like the letter "I" because the "I" shape is harder to bend.

Girders weigh 105 kg per metre of length.

## THE STRENGTH OF DIFFERENT SHAPES

The strength of a triangle comes directly from its shape. Unlike many other shapes the triangle is very strong. In fact, a triangle cannot be changed unless one of its joints or sides breaks.

Other shapes can be changed when pressed down.

To make rectangles and squares stronger a diagonal strut is used to turn the shape into two triangles, like this. This stops the rectangle or square from being pushed over.

strut

*The frame of a skyscraper is a series of trianges — the strongest shape there is.*

## CONSTRUCTION FACTS

A large team of construction workers are responsible for building the skyscraper, using drawings created by the architects and engineers. Some builders work the cranes to move and place materials, and others mix and pour concrete. Workers also connect steel beams, girders and columns together. The construction phase may take 2-3 years.

# RESISTING EARTHQUAKES

It is very important, particularly in certain parts of the world, to make sure that your skyscraper can withstand earthquakes. You will need a stiff **frame** made from beams, **columns** and concrete walls, and perhaps triangular steel **braces** for extra strength. A strong frame will keep your skyscraper safe in both high winds and earthquakes. Wind pushes on the building from above the ground but earthquakes push on the building from below the ground. During an earthquake the ground moves and the rest of the building has to move with it otherwise it falls down. Modern skyscrapers are strong and flexible, and can survive earthquakes that damage many lower buildings.

## SKYSCRAPER WORK

The DATA BOX on page 21 shows information about how the **Richter scale** is used to measure earthquakes.

The following numbers stand for different sized earthquakes. Can you put them in order of size from the smallest tremors to the most serious earthquakes?

| | | | |
|---|---|---|---|
| 2.8 | 3.55 | 3.05 | 2.42 |
| 2.57 | 3.0 | 2.21 | 3.4 |

The shape of this skyscraper in San Francisco helps it to withstand earthquakes.

## CHALLENGE QUESTIONS

1) Decide where each of these decimals should be placed on this line.

2.8    3.55    3.05    2.42    2.57    3.0    2.21    3.4

2    3    4

2) Round each of the decimals to the nearest tenth.
3) Now round each of the decimals to the nearest whole number.

*(You will find a TIP to help you with these questions on page 29)*

## SWAYING FACTS

The earlier skyscrapers, such as the Empire State Building, were built very solidly and even in very strong winds these buildings only sway about 50 cm at the top. Newer skyscrapers, however, are made with more flexible materials and are much taller so are designed to be able to sway up to 1.5 m at the top in extreme winds.

## THE RICHTER SCALE

12    Major or complete destruction; objects are thrown into the air, the ground is heavily shaken and distorted.

11    Few buildings remain standing; bridges and railways are destroyed; water, gas, electricity and telephones are out of action.

10    Ground badly cracked open and many buildings are destroyed. There are some landslides.

9    Huge earthquake, major damage and loss of life over a large region over 1000 km.

8    Great earthquake, great destruction, loss of life over several 100 km.

7    Major earthquake causes serious damage up to 100 km.

6    Damage to buildings within 10s of kilometres. Trees sway, some damage from collapsing and falling objects.

5    Feeling like a heavy truck has struck a building. People sleeping are woken.

4    Felt by people; shaking of objects.

3    Vibrations like those of heavy traffic.

2    Noticed only by sensitive people.

1    Recorded on local **seismographs** (machines that measure earthquakes), but usually not felt (microquakes).

## QUAKE FACTS

Large earthquakes can last for about 10-45 seconds. They are often followed by one or more smaller earthquakes, called 'aftershocks'. The aftershocks can cause some damaged buildings to collapse completely.

*When earthquakes occur in cities, it is often the older buildings that are damaged while the skyscrapers remain safe.*

**W**hen building a skyscraper with 100 floors or more it is vital to think about how people will get up and down the building. Not many people would want to climb 100 sets of stairs unless there was an emergency! You'll need to put in lifts or **elevators**. But you also must think about safety features. How can the building best be evacuated quickly and safely? If there is a power failure, or a fire, it may not be safe to use the lifts. Your building will need stairs as well. Where will you put emergency stairwells? How many will you have? Many tall buildings have a helicopter landing pad on the roof: it could be useful in an emergency.

## SKYSCRAPER WORK

A skyscraper has 150 storeys above ground level. There are 22 steps between each storey.

1) How many stairs would have to be climbed from the ground floor to reach floor
   a) 3?       e) 45?
   b) 4?       f) 50?
   c) 10?      g) 70?
   d) 16?      h) 100?

2) Each stair is about 16 cm high. Approximately how high would a 22-step flight of stairs be?

3) Use your answer to question 2 to help you **estimate** the height of 150 flights of stairs in metres.

## CHALLENGE QUESTIONS

Use the information in the DATA BOX on page 23 to help you answer these questions:

1) How long would it take a standard lift to travel (without stopping) from ground level to:
   a) floor 10?
   b) floor 25?
   c) floor 54?
   d) floor 72?
   e) floor 110?

2) How long would it take an express lift to travel (without stopping) from ground level to:
   a) floor 10?
   b) floor 25?
   c) floor 54?
   d) floor 72?
   d) floor 110?

3) How much faster is the express lift than the standard lift for each of the journeys above?

*(You will find a TIP to help you with these questions on page 29)*

## EMERGENCY FACTS

People are always trying to design better systems for evacuating people from high-rise buildings quickly and safely in an emergency. Ideas for how this can be done include external telescopic ladders and stairs; a rope device for people to tie around their waist and lower themselves down the outside of a building; and even emergency escape tubes. Many of these ideas are not suitable for very high towers or for elderly people or children. There are regulations in each city that specify the emergency safety measures that must be included in a new building.

**DATA BOX**

## LIFT SPEEDS

The distance between the floors of the skyscraper you are designing (called the floor-to-floor height) is 3 metres.

Your standard lifts travel about 6 metres per second.

Your express lifts travel about 10 metres per second.

*Emergency stairwells are usually very plain – after all, most people will never need to use them.*

## ELSHA OTIS

Most people don't want to climb hundreds of stairs each day. Commercial skyscrapers were not possible until 1853, when an American, Elisha Otis, invented a device to make lifts in tall buildings safe. The device was an emergency brake, which prevents lifts from free-falling if their mechanics fail. This gave people confidence that lifts were practical and safe for use. The first 'modern' lifts were steam-powered. Lifts today are **hydraulic** or electric.

# THE BUILDING PROCESS

**Y**our designs have been approved by architects and engineers and you must now start the difficult work of building the skyscraper. You will need lots of skilled people to help you. At first, you will need people who specialise in digging foundations; later you will need construction workers. When the building is finished, you will need electricians, plumbers and plasterers. It can take several years to build a skyscraper. You'll need to think carefully about the safety of the workers, as building a skyscraper can be a dangerous thing. Make sure that everyone working on the site wears a hard-hat and steel-toed boots to protect themselves.

## SKYSCRAPER WORK

It generally takes seven days to build each floor of a skyscraper.

Use the calendar on the right to help you answer these questions.

1) If the building work for the ground floor started on Feb 5th on which date will the:
   a) 2nd floor be completed?
   b) 4th floor be completed?
   c) 7th floor be completed?
   d) 9th floor be completed?
   e) 16th floor be completed?
   f) 20th floor be completed?

2) Estimate how long it would take to complete the:
   a) 52nd floor
   b) 104th floor

3) Which floor is being built on:
   a) 18th February?
   b) 27th February?
   c) 20th March?
   d) 1st May?

**FEBRUARY**

|    |    |    |    |    |    |    |
|----|----|----|----|----|----|----|
|    |  1 |  2 |  3 |  4 |  5 |  6 |
|  7 |  8 |  9 | 10 | 11 | 12 | 13 |
| 14 | 15 | 16 | 17 | 18 | 19 | 20 |
| 21 | 22 | 23 | 24 | 25 | 26 | 27 |
| 28 | 29 |    |    |    |    |    |

**MARCH**

|    |    |    |    |    |    |    |
|----|----|----|----|----|----|----|
|    |    |  1 |  2 |  3 |  4 |  5 |
|  6 |  7 |  8 |  9 | 10 | 11 | 12 |
| 13 | 14 | 15 | 16 | 17 | 18 | 19 |
| 20 | 21 | 22 | 23 | 24 | 25 | 26 |
| 27 | 28 | 29 | 30 | 31 |    |    |

**APRIL**

|    |    |    |    |    |    |    |
|----|----|----|----|----|----|----|
|    |    |    |    |    |  1 |  2 |
|  3 |  4 |  5 |  6 |  7 |  8 |  9 |
| 10 | 11 | 12 | 13 | 14 | 15 | 16 |
| 17 | 18 | 19 | 20 | 21 | 22 | 23 |
| 24 | 25 | 26 | 27 | 28 | 29 | 30 |

**MAY**

|    |    |    |    |    |    |    |
|----|----|----|----|----|----|----|
|  1 |  2 |  3 |  4 |  5 |  6 |  7 |
|  8 |  9 | 10 | 11 | 12 | 13 | 14 |
| 15 | 16 | 17 | 18 | 19 | 20 | 21 |
| 22 | 23 | 24 | 25 | 26 | 27 | 28 |
| 29 | 30 | 31 |    |    |    |    |

**JUNE**

|    |    |    |    |    |    |    |
|----|----|----|----|----|----|----|
|    |    |    |  1 |  2 |  3 |  4 |
|  5 |  6 |  7 |  8 |  9 | 10 | 11 |
| 12 | 13 | 14 | 15 | 16 | 17 | 18 |
| 19 | 20 | 21 | 22 | 23 | 24 | 25 |
| 26 | 27 | 28 | 29 | 30 |    |    |

*The site manager is in charge of a large team of workers, the machinery and the materials.*

## SAFETY FACTS

Building a skyscraper is dangerous, but today there are many rules to protect workers.

• Before the outside walls are built, the floors of the building are fenced to prevent workers from falling.

• Hard hats and steel-toed boots are always worn on the construction site.

• High winds sometimes cause construction to stop because it is too dangerous for the builders.

• When climbing on beams and **girders**, workers must use a safety rope to tie them to the building.

## SKYSCRAPER WHO'S WHO

Architects and engineers work together to design a skyscraper. It may take 1-2 years.

ARCHITECTS decide what the outside of the building will look like and how it will fit into the landscape surrounding it. They also design the layout of the inside space: how the rooms will be divided and where the lifts, corridors and toilets will be.

ENGINEERS make sure the building is strong enough to support itself, and the weight of the people, furniture and other things inside. They check that the building will be safe in strong winds and earthquakes. Engineers also ensure that the building will be properly heated, cooled, and that water and electricity are available where needed.

## CHALLENGE QUESTIONS

A skyscraper took 1456 days to design and build.

About how many weeks is this?
About how many months is this?
About how many years is this?

*(You will find a TIP to help you with this question on page 29)*

Congratulations! You've finally made it! Your skyscraper has been built. As you stand at the bottom and look up, you think is the most impressive building in the world. Other people seem to agree with you, and the offices and flats in the skyscraper have all been let. Within the building, the finishing touches have been made to the rooms and the furnishings are in place. Now you have to get approval from the safety inspectors before your building can finally be used. Soon people can begin to work in the offices on each floor or move into the flats there. You hope they will enjoy living and working in your skyscraper.

## SKYSCRAPER WORK

In the DATA BOX you will see information about the Sears Tower. Use the information to help you answer these questions:

1) In the whole building how many windows are there?
2) The antennae rises above the normal height of the building. How tall is the antennae?
3) If one metre is about 3.3 feet, give your answer to question 2 in feet.
4) If one tonne is 1000 kilograms, how many kilograms of steel were used to build the Sears Tower?
5) What is the **area** of the base of the tower?

Sears Tower, Chicago

## COIN FACT

Have you ever heard the story that dropping a coin from the top of a tall building could kill a person below? This is not true. A coin dropped from the tallest skyscraper will be travelling at the same speed when it hits the ground as a coin dropped from a 4-storey building. Whilst it may hurt you if it hit you on the head, it is very unlikely to be fatal!

The reason for this is because when an object falls a long distance, a point is reached where the air resistance (which slows a falling object down) is equal to the pull of gravity and the object stops gaining speed. It has reached 'terminal velocity' and won't go any faster.

## SWAY FACTS

Chandeliers and water in tubs or glasses on upper floors of skyscrapers can sometimes be seen to sway along with the building in high winds. Although the motion of the building causing this phenomenon is very safe, these visual cues may cause occupants to become uncomfortable and unsettled.

## DATA BOX · SEARS TOWER

Here is some information about the Sears Tower in Chicago, Illinois, USA.

| | |
|---|---|
| Height to the top of the building: | 442 metres |
| Height to the top of the antennae: | 527 metres |
| Weight of steel used: | 69,000 tonnes |
| Other materials used: | concrete, aluminium, glass |
| Foundation type: | Piles |
| Date completed: | 1974 |
| Number of floors: | 110 |
| Number of windows on each floor: | 146 |
| Number of lifts: | 106 |
| Base measurements: | 70 metres x 70 metres |

*Your skyscraper will attract a lot of interest. It will soon become a recognised landmark in the city, just like these skyscrapers in Denver, USA.*

## CHALLENGE QUESTIONS

Tall modern buildings sway side-to-side in strong winds. To estimate the number of metres that a skyscraper might sway in a very strong wind, find the height of the building in metres and then divide by 500.

The height of the skyscrapers below is given in metres. How much might the top of each sway? Give your answer in centimetres.

a) 500 m     c) 440 m     e) 415 m     g) 385 m
b) 450 m     d) 420 m     f) 390 m     h) 375 m

*(You will find a TIP to help you with this question on page 29)*

# TIPS FOR MATHS SUCCESS

PAGES 6-7

**Subtracting large numbers:**
When subtracting numbers with lots of digits, make sure that you line all the digits up so that the units line up with the units, tens with the tens, hundreds with the hundreds and so on.

PAGES 8-9

## CHALLENGE QUESTION

**Finding the difference between years:**
To find how many years between two dates, subtract the smaller year from the larger one. Make sure that you line all the digits up so that the units line up with the units, tens with the tens, hundreds with the hundreds and so on.

```
  1975
- 1931
    44    so 1975 is 44 years after 1931.
```

PAGES 10-11

The area of a shape is the amount of space inside the shape. It is measured in squares such as square centimetres ($cm^2$) or square metres ($m^2$).

**To find the area of a rectangle** multiply its length by its width.
Area = 8 x 4 = 32 $cm^2$

**To find the area of a triangle** multiply the base by the height and halve the answer.
Area = 8 x 4 ÷ 2 = 32 ÷ 2 = 16 $cm^2$

**The perimeter of a shape** is the distance all the way around the edge of it. To find the perimeter, first add the length and the width and then double your answer.
Perimeter = 4 + 8 + 4 + 8 = 24 cm

PAGES 12-13

**Rounding decimals to the nearest whole number:** remember that numbers ending in 5, 6, 7, 8 or 9 round up to the next whole number, and numbers ending in 1, 2, 3, 4 round down to the previous whole number.

## CHALLENGE QUESTION

You know that the length plus the width will be 100 m (half the perimeter). So choose pairs of numbers that add up to 100 (eg, 90 and 10, 80 and 20 etc) and multiply them to find the area.

The volume of a 3D shape is the space inside it. It is measured in cubes, such as centimetre cubes (cm³) or metre cubes (m³). The volume of a cuboid is found by multiplying the length by the width by the height.

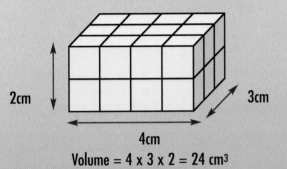

2cm

3cm

4cm

Volume = 4 x 3 x 2 = 24 cm³

have no equal sides or equal angles

have 2 equal sides and 2 equal angles

have all equal sides and all equal angles. The angles are all 60°.

## CHALLENGE QUESTION

When multiplying a number by 105, multiply the number by 100 and multiply it by 5 separately. Now add your two answers

8 x 105 = 8 x 100 = 800
8 x 5 = 40
800 + 40 = 840 so 8 x 105 = 840

Remember, to multiply a number by 100, move the digits two places to the left. We use zeros to fill any empty columns

63 x 100 = 6300

| Tth | Th | H | T | U |
|-----|-----|-----|-----|-----|
|     |     |     | 6 | 3 |
|     | 6 | 3 | 0 | 0 |

## CHALLENGE QUESTION

To find out the scale on a line, follow these steps.
1: Choose two adjacent (next to each other) numbers and find the difference between them.
2: Count how many small intervals (spaces) there are between these numbers.
3: Work out how much each of these intervals is worth.

## CHALLENGE QUESTIONS

When working out how long the lifts would take, first find out the distance it would travel for each journey, by multiplying the number of storeys by the height, 3 metres.

When you have found the distance, then, for the standard lift, divide by 6 or for the express lift, divide by 10.

## CHALLENGE QUESTION

Divide 1456 by
a) the number of days in a week
b) the number of days in a month
c) the number of days in a year

## CHALLENGE QUESTION

To divide a number by 500, you can divide by 5 and then divide by 100.

# ANSWERS ANSWERS ANSWERS

## PAGES 6-7

### SKYSCRAPER WORK

1) a) Taipai 101 Tower
   b) Empire State Building
   c) Sears Tower

2) a) 21
   b) 22
   c) 18
   d) 41
   e) 14

3) a) 10 m
   b) 17 m
   c) 67 m
   d) 24 m
   e) 15 m

### CHALLENGE QUESTIONS

1) a) 73    d) 68    g) 65
   b) 67    e) 72    h) 61
   c) 43    f) 66    i) 58

2) a) 876    d) 816    g) 780
   b) 804    e) 864    h) 732
   c) 516    f) 792    i) 696

## PAGES 8-9

### SKYSCRAPER WORK

1) a) almost 320 metres
   b) just over 440 metres

2) a) World Trade Center
   b) Empire State Building
   c) Taipai 101 Tower

3) a) Sears Tower
   b) Petronas Towers
   c) Empire State Building
   d) Empire State Building
   e) Taipai 101 Tower

### CHALLENGE QUESTIONS

1) a) 68    b) 1    c) 74    d) 42    e) 44

2) a) about 60 metres      c) about 10 metres
   b) about 60 metres      d) about 57 metres

## PAGES 10-11

### SKYSCRAPER WORK

1) Plot A 3600 m², Plot B 8800 m², Plot C 8100 m²,
   Plot D 3200 m², Plot E 10400 m²
2) a) 700 m²    b) 1600 m²
3) Plots A and D have perimeters of 240 m

### CHALLENGE QUESTION

a) 63 000 m²          d) 56 000 m²
b) 154 000 m²         e) 182 000 m²
c) 141 750 m²

## PAGES 12-13

### SKYSCRAPER WORK

1) Perimeters
   a) 138 m → 140  c) 186 m → 190  e) 174 m → 170
   b) 214 m → 210  d) 236 m → 240  f) 240 m → 240
2) Areas
   a) 1200 m²      c) 2400 m²      e) 2000 m²
   b) 2400 m²      d) 3200 m²      f) 3600 m²

### CHALLENGE QUESTION

1) a) 50m and 50 m      e) 45 m and 55 m
   b) 60 m and 40 m     f) 5 m and 95 m
   c) 80 m and 20 m     g) 49 m and 51 m
   d) 90 m and 10 m

## PAGES 14-15

### SKYSCRAPER WORK

1) a) a cuboid
   b) three cuboids, a cube and a square-based pyramid
   c) a hexagonal prism and a hexagonal-based pyramid
   d) a square-based pyramid
   e) a cylinder
   f) a triangular prism
2) a, e and f
3) a) 700 000 m³
   b) 800 000 m³

### CHALLENGE QUESTION

Building A has the greatest volume at 1 287 000 m³.
Building B is 1 098 000 m³ and Building C is
1 201 200 m³

## PAGES 16-17

### SKYSCRAPER WORK

a) -1      d) 5      g) 4
b) 2       e) -4     h) -5
c) -2      f) 6

### CHALLENGE QUESTION

Basement -3

# ANSWERS ANSWERS ANSWERS

## PAGES 18–19

### SKYSCRAPER WORK

1) A scalene    D scalene
   B equilateral    E isosceles
   C isosceles    F equilateral
2) Triangles C and D have right-angles
3) A 0    C 1    E 1
   B 3    D 0    F 3

### CHALLENGE QUESTION

a) 462 kg    c) 1155 kg    e) 2719.5 kg
b) 756 kg    d) 1533 kg

## PAGES 20–21

### SKYSCRAPER WORK

2.21   2.42   2.57   2.8   3.0   3.05   3.4   3.55

### CHALLENGE QUESTION

1)

2.21 2.42 2.57 2.8   3.0   3.05 3.4 3.55

2      3      4

| 2) | | 3) | |
|---|---|---|---|
| 2.8 to 2.8 | | 2.8 to 3 | |
| 3.55 to 3.6 | | 3.55 to 4 | |
| 3.05 to 3.1 | | 3.05 to 3 | |
| 2.42 to 2.4 | | 2.42 to 2 | |
| 2.57 to 2.6 | | 2.57 to 3 | |
| 3.0 to 3.0 | | 3.0 to 3 | |
| 2.21 to 2.2 | | 2.21 to 2 | |
| 3.4 to 3.4 | | 3.4 to 3 | |

## PAGES 22–23

### SKYSCRAPER WORK

1) a) 66    d) 352    g) 1540
   b) 88    e) 990    h) 2200
   c) 220    f) 1100

2) 352 cm or 3.52 m
3) About 525-528 metres

## PAGES 22–23 continued

### CHALLENGE QUESTION

| 1) | 2) | 3) |
|---|---|---|
| a) 5 seconds | a) 3 seconds | a) 2 seconds |
| b) 12½ seconds | b) 7½ seconds | b) 5 seconds |
| c) 27 seconds | c) 16.2 seconds | c) 10.8 seconds |
| d) 36 seconds | d) 21.6 seconds | d) 14.4 seconds |
| e) 55 seconds | e) 33 seconds | e) 22 seconds |

## PAGES 24–25

### SKYSCRAPER WORK

1. a) 25th Feb    d) 14th April
   b) 10th March    e) 2nd June
   c) 31st March    f) 30th June

2. a) 1 year
   b) 2 years

3. a) 1st floor    c) 6th floor
   b) 3rd floor    d) 12th floor

### CHALLENGE QUESTION

208 weeks
About 48 months
About 4 years

## PAGES 26–27

### SKYSCRAPER WORK

1) 16060 windows
2) about 85 m
3) About 280 feet
4) 69 million kilograms or 69,000,000 kg
5) 4900 m²

### CHALLENGE QUESTION

a) 100 cm    c) 88 cm    e) 83 cm    g) 77 cm
b) 90 cm    d) 84 cm    f) 78 cm    h) 75 cm

# GLOSSARY

**BRACE** Extra steel girders used to strengthen a structure.

**CAISSON** Part of the deep foundations of a building.

**COLUMNS** Vertical pillars that support the weight of the building.

**COMPRESSION** The act of pushing material together.

**ELEVATOR** Another name for a lift.

**FAÇADE** The outer front of a building that people see.

**FLOOR AREA RATIO (FAR)** The formula that some cities use to control the height of skyscrapers.

**FRAME** The structure that supports a building.

**GIRDER** A steel beam that is used to support other beams.

**HYDRAULIC** A mechanism which works by moving liquid.

**LOAD** The total weight of the building and everything in it.

**PILE FOUNDATION** Concrete 'stilt' structure below ground that supports the building.

**PLOT** The area of land available for building on.

**RAFT FOUNDATION** Concrete 'slab' structure below ground that supports the building.

**RESIDENTIAL** A building or area where people live.

**RICHTER SCALE** A scale used to measure earthquakes.

**SPIRE** The spike on top of a skyscraper. Skyscrapers are measured from the ground to the top of the spire.

**STOREY** A floor of a building.

**SEISMOGRAPH** A piece of equipment that measures earthquakes.

**SKYSCRAPER** General term used for very tall buildings.

**TENSILE** The act of pulling or stretching material.

**TORSION** Twist.

## MATHS GLOSSARY

**AREA** – the amount of space inside a flat (2D) shape. It is measured in square units such as $m^2$.

**EQUILATERAL TRIANGLE** – a triangle with all equal sides and all equal angles that are all 60°.

**ESTIMATE** – to find a number or amount that is close to an exact number.

**ISOSCELES TRIANGLE** – a triangle with 2 equal sides and 2 equal angles.

**NEGATIVE NUMBERS** – numbers that are less than zero, such as -4, -2, -12 etc.

**PERIMETER** – the distance all the way around the edge of a shape.

**PRISM** – a solid shape that is the same shape and size all along its length. If you slice through a prism parallel to its end face, the cut faces will all be the same size and shape as the end faces.

**PYRAMID** – a solid (3D) shape with a base, such as a square or hexagon. Its remaining faces are triangular and meet at a point.

**SCALENE TRIANGLE** – a triangle with no equal sides or equal angles.

**VOLUME** – the amount of space inside a solid (3D) shape. It is measured in cubic units such as $m^3$.

## PICTURE CREDITS
**Shutterstock**: 6 (inset, top) Norman Chan, 6 (inset, bottom) Yan Vugenfirer, 8-9 Jonathan Pais, 10-11 Leah-Anne Thompson, 12-13 luke james ritchie, 14-15 Jim Jurica, 16-17 Robert Cumming, 18-19 Wendy Kaveney Photography, 22-23 Ismael Montero Verdu, 24-25 Albo, 26 (inset) Wen-ho Yang. **Photodisc**: 6-7, 26-27. **Corbis**: 20 (inset). **FEMA**: 20-21 Robert A. Eplett.

Every effort has been made to trace the copyright holders, and we apologize in advance for any unintentional omissions. We would be pleased to insert the appropriate acknowledgements in any subsequent edition of this publication.